DRIVE

From Brokenness to Breakthrough — and Beyond

Dr. Kim Anderson

DRIVE

From Brokenness to Breakthrough — and Beyond

ISBN: 979-8-9990104-2-1

Scriptures are from the King James Version of the Bible, unless otherwise noted.

DEDICATON

To my beloved husband,

Thank you for your unwavering support, love, and encouragement.
You are my steady light through every foggy moment, a constant
reminder that I am never alone on this journey.

To my three beautiful children — **Jonathan, Jessica, and Jasmin**,
You carry greatness inside of you. No matter what life throws your
way, never stop moving forward. Every dream, every breakthrough,
every victory is already written in your story. You have the strength
to rise, the courage to endure, and the faith to overcome.

To my precious grandchildren,
May you always know that with God as your guide, no obstacle is
too great and no dream too big. Keep Him first, and He will lead you
through every fog, every fear, and into every promise.

THE BEST PART OF ME

You are, and always will be, the best part of me.

From left to right: Jessica, Jonathan, Jasmin

TABLE OF CONTENTS

FORWARD

As I sit down to write this foreword, I find myself reflecting on the incredible journey my wife, Dr. Kim Anderson, has undertaken—a journey marked by resilience, faith, and an unwavering commitment to her calling and *drive*.

Drive: From Brokenness to Breakthrough — and Beyond reflects who Kim truly is. Every time life tried to knock her down, something unshakable inside her rose up and refused to quit. Her story is raw, real, and full of moments where God's hand is unmistakable.

In these pages, you'll discover a roadmap for overcoming adversity, reclaiming your voice, and stepping into the fullness of who you were created to be. Although deeply personal, the words carry a universal truth. They come from her own journey, yet speak directly to the hearts of those she's touched—and those still waiting to hear her message.

I invite you to read with an open heart and a willing spirit. Allow Kim's story to ignite something within you, to challenge you, and to remind you that no matter where you are in your journey, breakthrough is possible.

With all my love – Bishop Gerald Anderson, Sr.

INTRODUCTION

To every woman who has ever cried in silence…

Who has smiled in public while breaking in private…

Who has loved deeply and been left empty...

This book is for **you**.

I know what it feels like to be broken. To give your all and still feel like you're not enough. To wonder why love didn't last, why your father wasn't there, why life dealt you a hand that felt so unfair. I've been in those dark places—questioning my value, my future, and even my identity as a woman of God. I've sat at the bottom emotionally, spiritually, and physically—trying to find the strength to get back up.

But something in me wouldn't let go.

That something was **drive**.

Drive is that sacred fire inside of you—the whisper that says, "There's more." It's what kept me going when the pain told me to stop. It's what carried me from brokenness to breakthrough... and then to something even greater: **beyond.**

This book is not just about pain. It's about **drive**—the inner push that refuses to let brokenness have the final say. It's about rising from what tried to bury you. It's about learning how to move forward, even when you don't feel ready. It's about realizing that your history does not define your destiny.

In these pages, I open up parts of my life that I once kept hidden— moments of abandonment, heartbreak, failure, and self-doubt. But I also share the **breakthroughs**, the **healing**, and the unexpected ways God used it all to shape something stronger, wiser, and more purposeful in me.

Whether you're in a dark place right now or walking out of one, I want you to know this: **your breakthrough is possible.** And not only that—it's only the beginning. There is a "beyond" waiting for you. A place where you no longer live from your wounds but from your healing. A place where your **drive** meets your **destiny**.

This is my story. But more than that, I pray it speaks to **yours**.

Let's begin.

CHAPTER ONE

THE POWER IN THE PIECES

Brokenness is not just a feeling—it's a condition of the soul. It's what happens when life breaks something inside of you that you didn't even know could shatter. For some, it's a single moment —like the loss of a loved one, a betrayal, or hearing words you can never un-hear. For others, it's not just one moment but a series of disappointments that slowly chip away at your confidence, your joy, and your sense of identity. For others, like me, it's a slow coming undone—like being reduced to a fraction in a math formula. You're still there, but not whole. Pieces of you scattered, simplified, divided—never quite adding up to what you once were.

Let's go deeper. You give your heart to tall, dark, and handsome—the one who says all the right things, makes you feel seen, wanted, even cherished. You believe the words, hold on to the moments, and dream a little about what the future could look like. But somewhere along the way, you start to notice the cracks—his actions don't match

1

his promises, his love feels conditional. What felt like safety no longer feels safe.

And then the truth hits: he wasn't there to love you—he was there because of the conveniences of you. The way you nurtured, the way you gave, the way you showed up for him in ways he never showed up for you. Maybe not just physically, but emotionally and spiritually. You were giving from a deep place, hoping that this time it was real, that this time love would stay. But he was only taking, drawing from your strength without ever pouring anything back in. That kind of heartbreak is hard to explain to others, especially when you're the one who stayed longer than you should have. But in that pain, in that soul-level ache, something shifts. You either collapse... or you rise.

And somewhere in the middle of that unraveling, you begin to see it: the power found in pieces. Not because you wanted to be broken, but because in the breaking, you discovered a strength you didn't know you had. A strength that only reveals itself when everything else falls away.

It doesn't happen all at once. The unraveling, I mean. It starts slowly—subtle at first, like a loose thread you don't think twice about tugging. A few things shift, some fall away, others crack beneath pressure you didn't notice building. Then, one day, you're standing in the middle of what feels like a collapse. And you think, *this is it*. This is the end.

But it's not.

Somewhere in the middle of all that breaking, something strange begins to take shape. You start to see it—not immediately, but gradually. A quiet power hiding in the rubble. Not because you ever wanted to be broken. No one wishes for that kind of pain. But because in the breaking, you found something you never would've discovered otherwise: a strength that doesn't make noise, but refuses to give up. A strength that only shows up when everything familiar falls away.

It's the kind of strength that can't be taught, only lived. You learn it not in your triumphs, but in the stillness after everything goes wrong. When the labels you wore no longer fit. When the plans you made go

3

Ka-boom. When there's no script to follow, and no one clapping at the end of your performance.

You're just… there. With the pieces.

And it's in those moments that you realize you're not as fragile as you thought. Yes, things broke. Yes, you're different now. But that doesn't make you less. In fact, it might make you more. Because when everything else is stripped away, what's left is the truest part of you, your authentic self. The part that survives. The part that keeps going, even without a map.

What if it was never about holding everything together? What if the falling apart was necessary—not as punishment, but as revelation? Maybe the pieces didn't scatter randomly. Maybe they were rearranging themselves into something better, something more aligned. You just couldn't see it from the middle of the mess.

Only in hindsight does the pattern emerge. Only after the pain can you see what it taught you.

Not that you're invincible. But that you're still here.

And maybe that's the real power in pieces. Not in putting yourself back the way you were, but in choosing who you'll become with what remains.

Rising doesn't happen all at once.

At first, it feels like crawling through the debris of what's left—your self-esteem, your trust, your sense of worth. You start to question everything: *"Was it ever real?" "How did I miss the signs?" "What does this say about me?"*

And those questions don't come quietly. They echo—especially late at night, when the world is asleep but your mind is wide awake.

What people often don't understand is that it's not just the loss of the person—it's the loss of the dream. The loss of what you thought you were building. The version of yourself you thought was finally being loved the right way.

But here's where the shift begins:

You stop chasing closure from someone who never had the capacity to give you clarity.

You stop trying to fix what you didn't break.

And you start—slowly, painfully—**reclaiming your voice.** Your value. Your boundaries.

Because brokenness might have been where the pain started, **but it doesn't have to be where the story ends.**

Take a moment to reflect on the experiences and beliefs that have shaped your journey:

1. What early experience in your life caused a deep sense of brokenness—and how has it shaped the way you see yourself today?

_____

_____

_____

2. Have you ever tried to fill the emptiness of brokenness with relationships, achievements, or distractions? What did you learn from that?

_____

_____

_____

3. What part of your story have you been afraid to face, and what would it mean for your healing if you allowed God—or truth—to meet you there?

_____

_____

_____

CHAPTER TWO

BREAKTHROUGH

Breakthrough begins in the moment you realize that where you are is not where you have to stay. It doesn't always come in a loud, dramatic shift. Sometimes, it's quiet. Subtle. It's the moment your spirit whispers, *"There has to be more than this."* It's the flicker of hope that shows up in a kind word, a timely message, or a sudden moment of clarity—when everything inside you wants to give up, but something tells you, *not yet*. And in that quiet shift, you begin to notice light slipping through the cracks, even while the darkness still feels overwhelming. You start to trust that the fight isn't over, even if you don't know how or when it will end. And maybe, just maybe, you don't need to know. Not yet.

Breakthrough is when you finally understand that being at the bottom doesn't mean you're finished—it means there's only one direction left to go: up. It's when your mindset begins to shift from *"Why me?"* to *"Watch me."* It's not just your circumstances that begin to change—it's *you*. The way you think. The way you speak to yourself. The way you finally understand that broken doesn't mean worthless.

8

It's like stepping out of the fog of self-doubt and into the clarity of self-worth. You realize that your value was never tied to what you lost, but to who you've always been—stronger than you thought, more capable than you imagined.

This is where rising begins—not because the struggle is over, but because you've made the decision that it won't define you. You stop measuring your worth by your scars and start seeing them as proof that you've survived. You stand up, even if your legs are shaking. You take another step forward, even if your heart is heavy. Breakthrough doesn't ask for perfection—it asks for persistence. It's knowing that even if you stumble, you're still moving in the right direction.

It's the moment you stop settling. You look around at rock bottom and declare, *"No. This is not how my story ends."* You stop accepting less than you deserve—not because you think you're perfect, but because you finally understand your story is still being written. The pages ahead may be blank in your notebook, but God has already written your future. You just have to live it out. Trust that every step you take, even the uncertain ones, is part of a much bigger plan. And even if the road ahead isn't always clear, the direction is—forward, toward what's meant for you.

You realize you have the power to rewrite the narrative. That's where true breakthrough lives—not in escaping the past, but in transforming it into the foundation for what comes next. You realize that you can do all things through Christ who strengthens you (Philippians 4:13). And in that moment, you don't just say it—you believe it. Deep down, you know that His strength is your strength. It's not just a verse—it's a truth that takes root in your soul.

So you get up. You dust yourself off. You wipe the tears from your eyes. You give yourself a moment of grace. Then, with a deep breath, you powder your face, look in the mirror, and speak life over yourself. *"Girl, you gone be alright. You are more than enough. Girl, you bad. You have it in you—everything it takes to become who you were always meant to be."* You say it loud. Say it proud. Say it like you mean it—because you do.

You've seen the darkness. You've faced the storm. And you've made it through. Now, you rise—not because it's easy, but because you can. Not because you have all the answers, but because you trust that with faith and persistence, you will get to where you're meant to be.

You've been through the fire, and you don't smell no smoke. Not a trace. The flames tried to burn you, tried to break you—but they couldn't. You stand here not consumed, but refined. Stronger. More powerful. More *you* than ever before.

You are not defined by what you've been through. You are defined by how you rise from it, how you fight through it, and how you keep moving forward. And girl—you are moving forward.

Take a moment to pause and go inward. Let these questions guide your thoughts as you process your own breakthrough:

1. What would change in your life if you truly believed that your lowest point was not the end, but the beginning of your breakthrough?

   _____

   _____

   _____

2. Where in your life do you need to stop settling—and start standing in the truth of who God says you are?

_____

_____

_____

3. What is one truth you need to start speaking over yourself

daily to remind you of your strength, your worth, and your

purpose?

_____

_____

_____

CHAPTER THREE

FINDING YOUR INNER DRIVE

Drive is a gentle, persistent push within you—a quiet yet constant reminder that there is more. It urges you to keep moving forward, even when you're uncertain, lost, fearful or facing challenges.

It's like an ever-present companion that doesn't let you rest, doesn't allow you to escape. It's not a sudden rush of energy or a brief flash of motivation, but a constant inner force that lingers with you. You wake up with it, carry it with you throughout the day, and lie down with it—always there, never letting go. It nudges you forward, urging you to move, each moment of the day—persistent and unwavering. Inner drive is like a fueled fire that refuses to burn out — it's a relentless, self-sustaining force that keeps you moving forward, even when the external world grows dim or the path becomes difficult. It's a deep, internal motivation that doesn't depend on outside factors to stay lit.

It's almost like an invisible engine inside you, constantly propelling you forward, no matter what's happening around you.

It's the quiet determination that keeps you going when others might stop, the voice that whispers, "Keep going, there's something greater ahead", which keeps you grounded in the pursuit of something larger than the obstacles at hand.

Before You Turn the Page:

1. What does your inner drive look like, and how has it shaped your journey so far?

_____

_____

_____

2. Can you recall a time when your inner drive kept you moving forward, even when the path was unclear?

_____

_____

_____

3. What kind of person do you want to become, and how can your inner drive support that transformation?

_____

_____

_____

CHAPTER FOUR

THE CALL TO KEEP GOING – A MOMENT FOR REFLECTION

I can remember a time when I had no idea where I was headed. I had just quit my well-paying job at Ford Motor Company, was in my first semester of nursing school, and then found out my teenage daughter was pregnant. To make matters worse, my husband at the time walked out, and I cried my heart out. I failed my medical-surgical course by a tenth of a point, adding to the weight of everything else. I had no financial stability, no resources, and the person who had promised to love and cherish me was no more. It felt like I was spiraling out of control, like I was trapped in a scene from *The Matrix*—watching my house, my car, my marriage, my family fall apart before my eyes. The weight of shame and guilt consumed me, making it hard to breathe, let alone see a way forward.

I went from a size 8 to a size 4 without any intention, not by choice or design—but simply because of everything else taking its toll on my body, soul, and mind. The stress, the overwhelm, the emotional chaos—it all drained me, and I barely had the energy to take care of myself, let alone anyone else. But in the midst of all that, there was this quiet, persistent inner voice that said, *Get up.* It wasn't loud or demanding; it was a soft but firm reminder that I couldn't stay down forever, that somehow, someway, I had to keep moving forward.

In the midst of the uncertainty, I began to sense a flicker of hope. I couldn't change the past, but I realized I still had the power to shape my future. Little by little, I started to pick up the pieces, one step at a time. I learned that resilience isn't about avoiding failure, but about finding the strength to rise again, no matter how hard it gets. And so, I moved forward—not with all the answers, but with the courage to keep going, trusting that each step would lead me to something better.

Let's take a step back and think about this:

1. Can you recall a moment when you chose to keep going, even when everything inside you told you to stop?

_____

_____

_____

2. What would it feel like to look back years from now and know I gave up too soon?

_____

_____

_____

3. How would your life change if you could embrace the call to
   keep going without hesitation, even in moments of doubt?

_____

_____

_____

CHAPTER FIVE

BREAKING THE CHAIN: HOW DOUBT, FEAR, AND PROCRASTINATION HOLD YOU BACK

I can recall how fear gripped me like a glove. Ford Motor Company had just notified me that they were closing, and I had to sign my name on a list to relocate to Chicago within the next two weeks. I had lived in Saint Louis, Missouri, my entire life, never traveling much outside of the occasional mid-winter convention. Not to mention, I had just finished decorating my 3-bedroom, 1.5-bath, 1,200-square-foot home — a place I had come to love and was now afraid to let go of. The thought of moving to Chicago terrified me. What if I hated it? What if I couldn't return, especially after leaving behind the home I had worked so hard to create? And then there was the worry about my children. They had never lived anywhere else; they were in 4th and 5th grade, and I couldn't imagine how they'd adjust to such a big change. It felt like a decision that couldn't be right. It was fear that said, *What if?* But faith said, *Even if.* I questioned everything, from the move to the very idea of uprooting my family and life. But deep down, I knew this was a moment I couldn't shy away from — even if fear was whispering doubts every step of the way. I was paralyzed by the fear of making the wrong decision, unsure if relocating to Chicago was the right choice. Fear whispered, *What if I fail?* I can remember talking to my Uncle Frank about it, and he said, "The cattle upon a thousand hills belong to God" (Psalms 50:10). He reassured me that if I let my home go and needed to return to St. Louis, the Lord would bless me with another one. While I knew what he was saying was scripturally true, I couldn't shake the anxiety. I tossed and turned all night, restless because I knew a decision had to be made. As the days passed, procrastination began to set in. I'd tell myself, *You don't have to decide right now. You can always do it tomorrow.* But deep down, I knew that every moment of delay made the decision feel harder. Procrastination has a way of convincing us that there's always more time — but the longer we wait, the heavier the weight of uncertainty becomes. It's a trap that keeps us stuck in indecision, feeding our fear and self-doubt, while delaying the very action we need to move forward. Procrastination is the continual avoidance of a task, fully aware that delaying it will only lead to worse outcomes. It's like passing over opportunities repeatedly — P.O.O.R. — choosing short-

term comfort over long-term success, and ultimately hindering your

progress.

Let's take a moment to process this:

1. What are the fears that hold me back from making decisions or taking action in my life?

_____

_____

_____

2. When I feel overwhelmed by a decision, what is the source of my hesitation? Is it fear of failure, fear of the unknown, or something else?

_____

_____

_____

3. How often do I find myself saying, "I'll do it tomorrow"?
   What are the underlying reasons I procrastinate?

_____

_____

_____

CHAPTER SIX

FAITH IN THE PROCESS

There are times in life when the journey feels unbearable. When you feel like you just can't take it anymore, when everything around you seems bleak, and where you are trying to go feels farfetched. You start to ask yourself, *"is it ever going to happen?"* and wonder if the dream you're chasing will ever become a reality. The road ahead looks clouded because of the delays, detours, and roadblocks, making it hard to see any clear way forward. What you see with the naked eye doesn't seem to align with the vision you hold, as things aren't coming together as you planned. In these moments, it's easy to question if you're on the right path, or if you'll ever reach the place you've been striving for.

In those very moments—when doubt sneaks in like a thief in the night—that faith in the process must rise up. Faith isn't about what you can see right now; it's about trusting in what you can't see yet. "It's not about having every piece of the puzzle in place; it's about trusting that as you move forward, the pieces will fall into place.

23

Even when it feels like the chips are stacked against you, and the way forward seems impossible, it's in these very moments that the strength of God empowers you—not just to overcome, but to emerge with courage and resilience.

Believe it or not, tests come to make us stronger. We often don't realize what we're truly made of until we are tested. It's through these trials that our true strength is revealed. For example, you won't truly understand the depth of forgiveness until you either have to give it or need it yourself. Or have you ever thought you had truly forgiven someone, only to see them again and relive the hurt? You thought you were over it, but in that moment, you realize you're not—'unforgiveness' still resides within your heart. It's in these moments that we discover how much deeper our healing and forgiveness still need to go. But as disheartening as it may be to realize that where you thought you were, you are not, remember— you are not alone. There are others who have walked this path, who understand what you're going through, and who are ready to help you find your way out.

So, keep pushing, pressing, praying, and believing. Stay focused— follow one course until successful. Stay on the wall, because you are doing a great work. Why come down? Don't give up now—you're at the brink of your blessing. Every step forward brings you one step closer.

Let's look inward for a moment:

1. Can you think of a time when your faith was tested, and how trusting the process helped you grow? How can you apply that faith to your current journey?

   _____

   _____

   _____

2. How has your faith influenced your decision-making in difficult situations?

   _____

   _____

   _____

3. In what ways have you witnessed faith in action, and how did it affect your perspective?

   _____

   _____

Dr. Kim Anderson

_____

CHAPTER SEVEN

LEARNING TO REST WITHOUT QUITTING

" Come unto me, all ye that labour and are heavy laden, and I will give you rest." – *Matthew 11:28 (KJV)*

There's a difference between quitting and resting.

Too often, we confuse the two. We think that if we slow down, we're falling behind. That if we stop to catch our breath, we're losing momentum. We live in a society that craves instant gratification— always rushing, yet going nowhere fast. We stay busy, but sometimes we're just busy doing nothing.

But in the Kingdom of God, rest is not weakness — it's wisdom. Even Jesus took time to rest, to pray, and to be alone with the Father. He modeled sacred pauses. On the sabbath day, God rested. After feeding the five thousand, Jesus withdrew to pray. After healing the man full of leprosy, He stepped away into the wilderness and prayed. Today, we call it *self-care*. But Jesus showed us that rest is *soul care*. Jesus doesn't just offer physical rest — He offers soul rest. The kind that quiets your thoughts, resets your mind, and realigns your purpose. Soul rest is rest for the inner part of you — the place where your drive comes from. When your soul is rested, you can keep going. You can drive, even without a clear destination.

I've learned in my journey — through the long nights, the painful setbacks, and the confusing detours — that rest is part of the drive. You cannot sustain forward motion without sacred pauses. And those pauses don't mean you're giving up — they mean you're trusting God to carry what you can't.

Scripture reminds us in 1 Peter 5:7 (KJV):

"Casting all your care upon Him; for He careth for you."

In the moments when I wanted to quit, God whispered to my heart:

"Trust me, Kim. I've got you. I will give you rest."

Let's reflect:

1. In what areas of your life have you been pushing so hard that you've forgotten to rest? *Where have you mistaken exhaustion for progress?*

_____

_____

_____

2. What would it look like for you to pause — not to quit, but to trust God with the weight you've been carrying?

_____

_____

_____

3. Could rest be the quiet space where your next breakthrough begins?

_____

_____

_____

CHAPTER EIGHT

EMBRACING SETBACKS AS STEPPING STONES

I vividly remember the moment I failed my first nursing class, Medical Surgical 1. It was just a tenth of a point. I cried—uncontrollably—and then I cried again. I beat myself up over it, wondering how this could have happened. How could I have failed? I felt so ashamed. It was a struggle knowing that while my peers moved ahead, I was left behind. I cried because I was depending on this class to move forward, to keep going.

I had so much at stake. I had a four-bedroom, 2.5-bath home with a 3-car garage to pay for, along with car payments, utilities, groceries, and two daughters who were depending on me. During this time, my son was residing with his father. On top of it all, my marriage was going through a tough time, and my 14-year-old daughter was pregnant. It felt overwhelming. I could hardly make sense of it all. I was holding on to the hope that completing nursing school would give me the financial stability I desperately needed.

But as painful as it was, that failure became a catalyst for growth. It forced me to reassess my approach, build more resilience, and develop a deeper sense of determination. I realized that failure wasn't the end, but rather an opportunity to learn, adapt, and push forward with even greater focus. I was hired as a nurse extern at St. Mary's Hospital which was walking distance from my home. They allowed me to write my own work schedule. So, I worked 40 hours a week for two weeks, and then for the other two weeks, I would not work and use that time to study. I did this for the remainder of the nursing program. I re-enrolled, retook Medical Surgical 1, and ended the course with a B.

During this time, my daughter had my beautiful granddaughter, whom I call Pooh Bear. I wouldn't trade her for anything, and I wouldn't give her back if you paid me. The first year of her life, both her dad's side of the family and my family gave such a huge baby shower that I didn't have to make a single purchase. Things just began to fall into place, piece by piece. When I would sit in my bed studying, Pooh Bear would sit next to me. When I turned the page in my book, she would turn hers.

This setback was for my comeback. I continued with the nursing program, and sure enough, the Lord allowed me to graduate with honors. And who did I hold in my arms on graduation day? Pooh Bear.

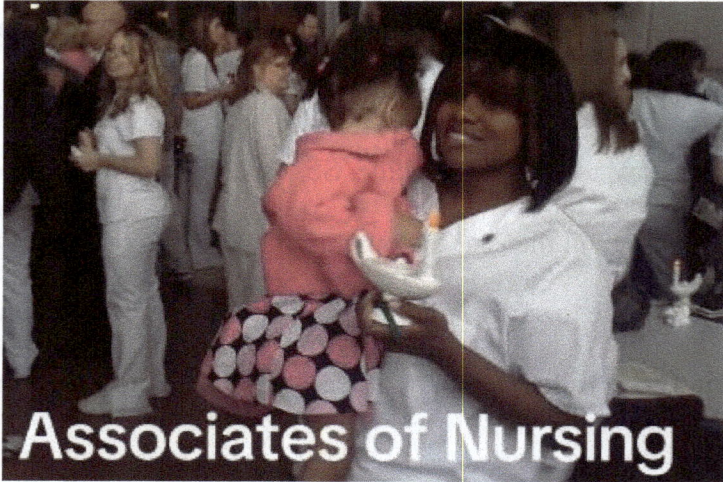

When I look back over my life, I wouldn't change a thing. It was through the storm and the rain that I discovered what God had put in me.

Let's take a brief pause and evaluate:

1. How did I initially react to the setback in my life, and what could I have done differently in my response?

_____

_____

_____

2. What did this setback teach me about myself, my skills, or my limitations?

_____

_____

_____

3. What is the biggest takeaway from this experience that I can apply to other areas of my life?

_____

_____

_____

CHAPTER NINE

THE POWER OF CONSISTENCY

I would like to take a moment to talk about the Power of Consistency. You might feel like your efforts are small or insignificant, but I want to remind you that slow and steady truly wins the race. When I think about where I am now in my career, I must admit it wasn't an overnight journey. It took ten years of starts, stops, and countless do-overs to get here. Progress wasn't always linear, but every step—no matter how small or uncertain—brought me closer to where I wanted to be. Success isn't about how fast you move; it's about your ability to endure. I know it may be easier said than done, but nothing worthwhile comes easy. When you've had to fight for it—pouring in sweat, blood, and tears, sacrificing sleep, and even being willing to give up your life for it—that's when the reward becomes truly meaningful.

You really don't focus on the hill you're climbing; instead, you focus on the climb itself. It's about embracing the journey, one step at a time, and finding strength in each moment of progress.

Just like the climb, consistency is about showing up every day and putting one foot in front of the other, even when the path feels steep. No matter what, you remind yourself: push forward, move now, get up. It's not about perfection or speed, nor is it about comparing yourself to others, because each person's course or journey is unique. While we may all have a similar destination, the routes we take can be vastly different. Some may encounter roadblocks, other detours, and some may even face delays like a flat tire.

What I'm trying to say is this: whether you're dealing with mounting debt, unemployment, or financial struggles; battling chronic illness or mental health challenges; caring for a loved one with serious needs; dealing with divorce, a breakup, or conflict with family and friends; experiencing repeated failures in your career, education, or personal goals; feeling isolated and unsupported; struggling to meet society's or your own expectations; navigating the demands of parenting; waiting for delayed success; fearing the unknown; or mourning the loss of a loved one, a job, a home, or a dream—the message remains the same: keep going. These obstacles might slow you down, but they don't have to stop you nor define your destination. Stay committed to the journey and refuse to give up because every step forward—no matter how small—brings you closer to what's ahead.

Let's pause for a moment to consider where we stand:

1. What specific challenges or circumstances are making me feel overwhelmed right now?

_____

_____

_____

2. What lessons might I learn from this experience, even if it's hard to see them now?

_____

_____

_____

3. How can I break my goal into smaller, more manageable steps to make progress less overwhelming?

_____

_____

_____

CHAPTER TEN

REDEFINING SUCCESS: WHAT DOES IT REALLY MEAN TO YOU?

In society, success is often defined by material possessions and status: one's social class, race, the home you live in, the car you drive, the money in your bank account, credit scores like FICO and VantageScore, level of education, or being part of the elite. But I see success differently.   Success isn't a one-size-fits-all concept; it's deeply personal and unique to each individual. After all, we don't all come from the same walk of life, nor do we have access to the same opportunities. You've probably heard the terms "privileged" and "underprivileged," right? Let's be clear: this isn't about making excuses; it's about reflecting on the diverse paths we take to find our own definitions of success.

For example, my grandfather dropped out of school in the 8th grade to help support his family, and my grandmother left school in the 3rd grade to wash clothes with her mother. At just 13 years old, she married my grandfather, who was 21 at the time. Despite their limited education and resources, they successfully raised eight

37

children with very little money. My grandfather worked as a butler, and alongside him, my grandmother worked as a maid. Later, he drove taxi cabs, cleaned offices, and eventually retired from the railroad. His last job was as a school bus driver. Through it all, he had a love for fishing, which provided him with a peaceful escape from the demands of life. My grandma ensured her children never missed a meal or went to bed hungry. They both taught their children the value of hard work, perseverance, and the importance of family. Similarly, my mother married my father at 17. Although she graduated from O'Fallon Technical High School, I vividly remember her cleaning the homes of what we called "rich folks." We would ride the Bi-State Bus to these homes, which were filled with the finest things. While our house on 5246 Wabada Avenue in the heart

of the city needed plenty of fixing, it also taught us valuable lessons in resilience. At first, we did not have a working toilet, so we had to use a bucket to relieve ourselves and walked a few blocks to my grandmother's house when we had to do number two. We heated the house with a wood-burning furnace, and whenever the house grew cold, my siblings and I took turns heading down to the basement to add wood to the fire. Despite the challenges, my mom did an incredible job raising us. She had six children, though one of them tragically passed away after a house fire. Through it all, she remained strong, ensuring we were loved and cared for, even in the toughest of times. We never went hungry, were never evicted, and though we were raised in poverty, her love, prayer life, faith in God, and determination gave us a strong foundation.

Out of her five children—three girls and two boys—she raised a family of achievers. None of her five children dropped out of high school, joined a gang nor went to prison. Her oldest daughter, Dr. Donita Lester, became the first in our entire family to earn a doctoral degree and authored the devotional "Spiritual Impartations by God." I pursued dual certification as a Family Nurse Practitioner and a

Psychiatric Nurse Practitioner, and later earned my Doctor of Nursing Practice degree, and my youngest sister, Evangelist and Missionary Lavone Morris, earned a master's degree and owns two successful businesses: Priced Just Right Fashion and Taxes by Lavone. My two younger brothers have also achieved remarkable success. One is a music producer, a minister of music at a local church, a real estate owner, a devoted husband, and an exemplary father. The youngest works in public transit and is also a loving husband and wonderful father.

For me, success isn't about fitting into society's cookie-cutter mold. It's about resilience—the ability to get back up when you fall. It's about starting a task and seeing it through to completion. Success is deeply personal, and it's so much more than societal metrics or material gains. There's no blueprint or guaranteed path to success, except through God. As Proverbs 3:13-15 (ESV) says, *"Blessed is the one who finds wisdom, and the one who gets understanding, for the gain from her is better than gain from silver, and her profit better than gold. She is more precious than jewels, and nothing you desire can compare."* True success, from the Lord's perspective, is rooted in wisdom, understanding, and a heart aligned with His will.

I want to challenge you to move beyond society's definition of success and create your own. My urgent question for you is this: What do you want to do, become, or achieve? Perhaps an even more important question is, what do you want to stop doing? Are you ready to stop being a people pleaser? Are you ready to define success on your own terms and live a life true to yourself?

Reflection Questions:

1. How do you currently define success in your life? Does this definition align with your personal values and goals?

   _____

   _____

   _____

2. Are there habits, relationships, or mindsets you need to let go of to pursue your definition of success?

   _____

   _____

   _____

3. What small, consistent actions can you begin today to move
    closer to your goals?

_____

_____

_____

CHAPTER ELEVEN

DRIVEN BY PURPOSE, NOT PRESSURE

Purpose is what you are divinely designed to do in the natural. I like to think of purpose as the opposite of pressure.

Take a car, for example — its sole purpose is to be driven. It was built to move, not to sit idle. But what I had to learn is that I am not built to run someone else's race. I had to stop comparing myself to others and start seeking what God created me to do.

Many times, when we don't know our purpose, we start imitating others. We chase what looks successful instead of what's meant for us. And before we know it, we're living under pressure — unfulfilled, overwhelmed, and out of alignment with who we truly are.

And if we're not careful, we begin to look at others through a critical lens — becoming judgmental, nitpicking what they're doing, all while avoiding the real work of discovering what we are called to do. That pressure builds into frustration, but purpose brings peace.

Dr. Kim Anderson

Knowing your lane allows you to cheer others on while staying focused on your own.

The Bible says we were created in His own image and made for His pleasure (Revelation 4:11). That means we must go to Him — our Creator — for the answer to what we are meant to do.

For example, if I were given a shoe and didn't know what to do with it, I would go to the shoemaker. The shoemaker would tell me, "Put it on your foot — it's designed to protect you as you walk." In the same way, only God can fully reveal our purpose. He knows what He placed inside of us, and why.

The moment we begin to discover our **"why"** — the reason we were created — pressure begins to lift. It's like opening a tightly sealed jar. Before it's opened, there's resistance and pressure built up inside. But once it's opened, there's a release — a sense of relief. That's what purpose does: it relieves the pressure of performance, comparison, and confusion.

So, I initially didn't know what I was supposed to do. I was searching, uncertain, and honestly, just going through the motions. But the Lord, in His wisdom, moved me away from my family and my comfort zone — not to punish me, but to get my attention. It was

44

in that unfamiliar space, away from the noise and distractions, that I began to truly seek Him and hear His voice.

Sometimes God has to disrupt our familiar to help us discover our purpose. It's not always easy, but it's necessary. Comfort can keep us stagnant — but purpose will push us forward.

Let's Reflect:

1. Am I living in alignment with *my* purpose, or am I simply responding to outside expectations and pressures?

   _____

   _____

   _____

2. In what areas of my life have I felt the need to imitate others instead of seeking God's direction for myself?

   _____

   _____

   _____

3. What is one intentional step I can take this week to move closer to discovering or walking fully in my God-given purpose?

   _____

   _____

   _____

CHAPTER TWELVE

BUILDING RESILIENCE: BOUNCING BACK STRONGER AFTER ADVERSITY

B uilding mental toughness helps you bounce back stronger after adversity by equipping you with the tools to cope effectively with challenges.

It is suggested that the four components—control, commitment, challenge, and confidence—are the key elements that drive mental toughness. Control is the ability to manage one's emotions when life is turbulent and keep anxiety in check. Commitment involves staying on course despite obstacles. Challenge is the mindset of viewing difficulties not as setbacks, but as opportunities for personal growth and adaptation in an ever-changing world. Confidence is the belief in oneself and one's destiny, even in the face of setbacks, and the determination to keep moving forward, step by step (Yin et al., 2017).

After failing my RN certification, I was devastated. I had been hired to work on the telemetry unit, but after receiving the disappointing news, I had to call my nurse manager and share that I hadn't passed.

She informed me that they could no longer hold the position they had offered and asked me to report to the rehab unit to work as a tech instead.

At the time, I felt both disappointed and uncertain about what this change meant for my future. However, little did I know, this shift would lead to something beautiful—something I never could have anticipated. While working on the rehab unit, I met a patient who quickly grew very fond of me. She asked if I would care for her in her home. At first, I hesitated, unsure of how to navigate home care, but her persistence eventually convinced me to give it a try.

For several months, I spent 8 hours a day, 5 days a week sitting with her in her home, while also maintaining my position at St. Mary's, albeit with reduced hours. Looking back, it turned out to be one of the greatest blessings of my life. During those hours, I was able to study for my RN certification again, and in time, I passed the exam. When I called my manager, Beth, to share the good news, she responded with, "I knew you would. Report to the telemetry unit tomorrow." That moment was so much more than just a return to my original role—it was a powerful testament to control (don't give up),

47

commitment (open your books and start studying again), challenge (you are still capable, get back in the race), and confidence (that he who began a good work in you is faithful and just to finish it Philippians 1:6 KJV)!

Returning to my original role not only marked a significant moment in my nursing journey, but it also prompted me to expand my business, Kind Caregivers. As I transitioned back into the telemetry unit, I realized that I needed to hire additional employees to keep up with the growing demand for care. This allowed me to provide 24-hour service for my patient, ensuring that she continued to receive the care she needed while I worked on my career and business. Finish it—come on, future Registered Nurse!

Perhaps you might feel that you possess one, two, or maybe even three of these components, or perhaps you feel you have none at all. However, the good news is that mental toughness can be learned. Learning mental toughness involves developing the four key components—control, commitment, challenge, and confidence—through practice and mindset shifts. Here are some ways to build each of these traits:

1. **Control**: Practice emotional regulation by staying calm during stressful situations. Techniques like mindfulness, deep breathing, and journaling can help you manage emotions and reduce anxiety.

2. **Commitment**: Strengthen your perseverance by setting clear, achievable goals and staying focused on them despite obstacles. Break big tasks into smaller steps and celebrate progress along the way.

3. **Challenge**: Change your perspective on difficulties by viewing them as opportunities for growth rather than threats. Embrace challenges as chances to learn and adapt, and remind yourself that growth often comes from discomfort.

4. **Confidence**: Build self-belief by reflecting on past successes and reminding yourself of your strengths. Set small wins that reinforce your abilities and practice positive self-talk to counteract doubts.

Through consistent effort and practice, these components can become stronger, helping you build greater mental toughness over time.

Let's reflect:

Control:

- How do I typically respond to stressful or challenging situations?

_____

_____

_____

Commitment:

- Have I ever given up on a goal because of obstacles? What made me decide to quit?

_____

_____

_____

Challenge:

- How do I usually view difficulties or failures—do I see them as roadblocks or opportunities to learn?

_____

_____

_____

Confidence:

- How do I talk to myself when things aren't going well? What would happen if I replaced negative self-talk with positive affirmations?

_____

_____

_____

CHAPTER THIRTEEN

THE ART OF SAYING NO: SETTING BOUNDARIES TO PROTECT YOUR ENERGY

L earning to say "no" is essential for maintaining focus and protecting your drive, even though it may feel difficult at times. There comes a point in life when you can no longer be the "yes ma'am, yes sir, I can do that for you" type of person. You can't be everything to everybody—only Jesus could do that. It's natural to feel like you're letting people down, and at first, your family and friends may not be receptive. Believe me, I've been there. But hold fast—they will adjust. When you have your eyes on a prize, staying focused means eliminating every distraction that drains your time, energy, and resources. You must adopt the "by any means necessary" attitude that the late Malcolm X embodied. Keep your focus on what truly matters to achieve your goals.

Setting boundaries is vital because it takes discipline to achieve what you have set out to do. There's a saying: you cannot have your hand in too many fires at the same time. It's like a working parent trying

51

to manage a full-time job, cook dinner during a work call, help their child with homework, and respond to urgent emails all at once. This often leads to feeling overwhelmed, making mistakes at work, and missing out on quality time with their child.

For someone pursuing their goals, this behavior can be detrimental. Trying to juggle too many responsibilities at once stretches your energy too thin, leaving you less effective in each area. It can delay progress, create unnecessary stress, and even lead to burnout. Setting clear boundaries allows you to channel your energy into the tasks that truly matter, keeping you aligned with your goals and on track for success.

Stop right here, let's have a moment of truth:

1. What distractions in your life are currently preventing you from focusing on your goals?

   _____

   _____

   _____

2. How can you start setting boundaries to protect your time, energy, and resources?

_____

_____

_____

3. Who might struggle to understand your new boundaries, and how can you communicate your intentions to them effectively?

_____

_____

_____

CHAPTER FOURTEEN

HARNESSING THE POWER OF POSITIVE

SELF-TALK

As children, we often said, "Sticks and stones may break my bones, but words will never hurt me," as a defense mechanism when others called us names. However, the truth is, that phrase wasn't entirely accurate. Words are incredibly powerful and can leave a lasting impression, shaping thoughts and emotions long after they are spoken.

If negative words can linger and shape our thoughts, imagine how much more impactful positive words can be. What we speak from our mouths shapes our actions, our mindset, and our ability to move forward. For this reason, it is essential to speak only what we believe, even when what we are believing for has not yet come to fruition. The Bible reminds us that the power of life and death is in the tongue, and we will have what we declare. So, choose to speak life and watch it manifest.

Growing up, I often said, "I am a King's kid, and the only thing a King's kid doesn't have is the things he or she doesn't want." This simple affirmation reminded me of my identity and the abundance available to me as a child of God. It shaped my mindset to focus on what I believe, be thankful for what I have, and pursue the limitless possibilities of what I could achieve and receive.

Remember, when we speak, our words go out into the atmosphere, take form, and do what we've told them to do — not what someone else has. So, speak what you see.

Stop, pause, and reflect:

1. How have words, both positive and negative, shaped your thoughts or emotions in the past? Can you think of a time when someone's words stuck with you?

   _____

   _____

   _____

2. What are some affirmations or positive statements you can speak over your life to remind yourself of your potential and identity?

   _____

   _____

_____

3. How does the idea of speaking life into existence align with your faith or personal beliefs? In what areas of your life could you speak more hope and positivity into your future?

_____

_____

_____

CHAPTER FIFTEEN

THE ROLE OF PATIENCE: TRUSTING THE TIMING OF YOUR JOURNEY

Have you ever heard the saying, "Good things come to those who wait, but not to those who wait too late"? I see it a little differently. Just because things don't happen according to our own timeline doesn't mean they won't happen at all. Where you are right now is exactly where you need to be, and when the time is right, you'll reach your final destination. I know how it feels to be frustrated by waiting—wondering if you've waited long enough or if things are just not going to happen for you. I remember when I made the decision to return to college and become a family nurse practitioner. I eagerly applied and waited for my acceptance letter, but it felt like it was taking forever. I heard that admissions were based on GPA, and I worried that I might end up on the waitlist. I even called the university, and they simply said, "We don't know yet." So, I started applying to other schools. I got accepted to Western Governors University for a Master's in Healthcare

Administration, but honestly, I wasn't sure it was what I truly wanted.

Then one day, I came home from work and found a letter in my mailbox. It was the acceptance letter I had been waiting for: "Congratulations, you've been accepted into the Family Nurse Practitioner program." As I read those words, with tears in my eyes, I heard a voice say, "This is the program you wanted all along." Talk about joy and gratitude in full effect—it was a moment of pure, overwhelming thankfulness.

I share this with you because I don't want you to give up or lose hope. Just because things aren't happening right now, or as quickly as you'd like, doesn't mean they won't happen at all. Stay focused and remember to follow one course until successful. Stay the course, trust the timing, and keep moving forward. Proverbs 3:5-6 (KJV) reminds us to *"Trust in the LORD with all thine heart; and lean not unto thine own understanding. In all thy ways acknowledge him, and he shall direct thy paths."* The right opportunity will come when it's meant to. Trust that God's timing is perfect and that He is guiding you toward what is best for your life.

Trusting with all thine heart requires us to give it to Him, every ounce of it, and leave it there. And when we find ourselves taking it back from Him, we must stop and give it right back to Him. Letting go and surrendering completely is part of the process of trusting Him fully.

I know we want all of the details at least I did. I know we want to visually see how it will turn out, or better yet, have a computer printout to show us the final result. But that's not how it goes. We are called to trust, even without seeing the entire picture. God often works in ways we don't expect, and part of the journey is learning to have faith in His plan, even when it's not fully revealed to us.

Take a moment to consider:

1.   How do I typically respond when things don't unfold according to my expected timeline, and what can I learn from these experiences to stay more patient and focused?

_____

_____

_____

2.   In what areas of my life do I need to trust that the right opportunities will come at the perfect time, even if they don't happen right away?

_____

_____

_____

3.   What is one action I can take today to stay focused on my goals and keep moving forward, even if I haven't yet seen the results I'm hoping for?

_____

_____

_____

CHAPTER SIXTEEN

THE STRENGTH IN VULNERABILITY

I want to share a moment of vulnerability I experienced when I asked for forgiveness. Maybe you've had a vulnerable moment of your own—whether it was expressing your feelings of love, admitting you don't have all the answers, revealing your age when you returned to college, discussing financial difficulties, stepping outside of your comfort zone, or even challenging the stigma around seeking professional counseling. For me, asking for forgiveness became one of those defining moments. These moments can feel incredibly exposing, but they are often essential for our growth and connection with others.

Through my own journey of vulnerability and growth in Christ, one of the most important lessons I've learned is the power of reconciliation—even when the response is not what I expect. I found myself apologizing to someone, but their response wasn't what I had hoped for. The Bible teaches us that if we come to the altar and remember that someone has something against us, we should leave our gift at the altar and go reconcile with them first (Matthew 5:23 KJV). This principle stuck with me, reminding me that the act of seeking forgiveness and pursuing reconciliation isn't about the immediate response we receive, but about obeying God's call for peace and healing. Even when the outcome isn't as we expected, vulnerability in this process helps us grow spiritually and deepen our relationships.

For me, asking for forgiveness was truly an act of vulnerability. On one hand, I wanted to make things right because I wanted to be in right standing with God and follow His Word. But on the other hand, there was that fear of how the other person would react, especially if their response wasn't what I had hoped for. Sometimes, you may not even realize there's an issue, but the other person has been silently holding something against you—though it's evident in their behavior. They might even say, "You've always done this" or "You've always done that," leaving you unaware of the hurt they've carried. Yet, despite this, God still calls us to go to them and seek reconciliation. Though it can be frustrating and painful when the response isn't what we want, these are the moments where God calls us to act in obedience. Reconciliation isn't just about resolving the issue at hand;

it's about healing hearts and fostering peace, even when it's difficult. After all, when we forgive, we free the prisoner—and that prisoner is us.

Consider these questions:

1. In what areas of my life am I avoiding vulnerability, and how might embracing it help me grow or connect more deeply with others?

   _____

   _____

   _____

2. When I've been vulnerable in the past, what positive outcomes or lessons have I learned, and how can I apply those insights moving forward?

   _____

   _____

   _____

3. What fears or insecurities prevent me from showing vulnerability, and how can I challenge myself to be more open and authentic in those moments?

   _____

   _____

   _____

CHAPTER SEVENTEEN

CREATING YOUR PERSONAL VISION: MAPPING THE PATH TO YOUR IDEAL FUTURE

When I look back at where I am today, I realize that my path wasn't always crystal clear. But the key was to start, even if the full picture hadn't emerged yet.

Leaving my job at Ford, I faced a major decision. With financial obligations and children to raise, I knew I needed to be practical about my next steps. Instead of jumping into a four-year program right away, I chose to complete a two-year associate's degree in nursing. It felt like the smarter, more manageable choice, considering my circumstances.

Once I had that foundation, I took a year off, then pursued an accelerated Bachelor of Science in Nursing program, completing it in just 13 months. I didn't stop there. Another year off, and then I enrolled in a Family Nurse Practitioner program, finishing it in 18 months. Following that, I took another year off to rest and regroup, but then I returned to school to pursue my Psychiatric Nurse Practitioner degree.

I wasn't done yet. After just a six-month break, I went after my Doctor of Nursing Practice degree. Each step built upon the last, and though the journey was long and sometimes uncertain, I was always clear on one thing: I was working toward something greater.

Reflecting on My Path:

Start where you are. Often, we hesitate to begin because we don't see the whole picture. But you don't need to know every step—just take the first one.

Adjust your path as life unfolds. Plans change, priorities shift, and opportunities emerge. Be flexible enough to take advantage of them when they come, even if it means stepping away from one thing to pursue another.

Take your time, but don't stop. Life will always have interruptions—whether they're financial, personal, or simply unexpected. But consistency over time leads to progress.

Vision evolves. The vision you start with might change along the way, and that's okay. Keep your eyes on the big picture, but be open to adapting as you move forward.

The path I took wasn't easy, but by mapping out a vision and taking one step at a time, I've been able to create a career and life that align with my values and goals. Hopefully, drawing from my shared experience of navigating uncertainty and taking steady steps toward my goals will help you define your long-term vision and align your actions with it. If you start today, even if it's just one small step, you'll find yourself further along tomorrow than you were yesterday.

Let's take a moment to ponder:

1. What is the first step I can take today toward achieving my long-term vision, even if I don't have the entire plan figured out?

_____

_____

_____

2. In what areas of my life do I need to practice patience and persistence, knowing that my goals will take time to manifest?

_____

_____

_____

3. What limiting beliefs or doubts do I need to release in order
    to fully pursue my dreams and trust the process of my
    growth?

_____

_____

_____

CHAPTER EIGHTEEN

THE INFLUENCE OF ENVIRONMENT: SURROUNDING YOURSELF WITH PEOPLE WHO FUEL YOUR FIRE

I t's true that birds of the same feather flock together—our environment and the people we surround ourselves with can have a profound impact on our drive and success. When I was pursuing my nursing degree at Valparaiso University, I found that the collective energy of other motivated students helped fuel my own commitment to my goals.

One thing that really motivated me during my time there was the library, which stayed open until midnight. After finishing my shift at St. Mary's Hospital, I would drive straight there to study. What made it especially inspiring was seeing so many other students, some I'd never met, up late studying as well. You'd see small groups huddled together in corners, others focused in study rooms, and some just sitting in the open areas. Even though we didn't know each other, being surrounded by others who were equally dedicated helped me feel connected and reminded me that I wasn't alone in the effort.

The environment you immerse yourself in plays a huge role in shaping your mindset and motivation. Valparaiso University offered a community of like-minded individuals, even if you didn't know them personally. Just seeing others pushing toward their goals at the same time creates a sense of solidarity and shared purpose. It's often easy to feel isolated during intense study sessions, especially in a demanding field like nursing, but when you're surrounded by others who are equally dedicated, it can be energizing and reassuring. The fact that I was not alone in the late hours of study created an unspoken sense of accountability. Although I was not working directly with them, just being in that shared space with a collective focus likely kept my motivation high. That environment nurtured my own drive by showing me that others, too, were putting in the effort. Creating such an environment, whether at school, work, the gym, or even home, is incredibly important for staying focused on one's goals. This can be achieved by surrounding oneself with people who support and encourage personal aspirations. Additionally, cultivating a physical space that promotes concentration—whether that's a quiet corner, a well-organized study room, or a creative workspace—can also be helpful.

During my preparation for the Family Nurse Practitioner license, I even had a study buddy with whom I created a 30-day study calendar. Each day, we focused on specific clinical concepts, ensuring that we didn't move on to the next concept until we fully understood the material. The content we covered was extensive, consisting of the clinical knowledge needed to provide primary care to patients across the entire lifespan—prenatal, pediatric, adolescent, adult, and older adult populations. It included areas like patient assessment, diagnosis, preventative measures, health promotion, and management of common conditions across all age groups, as well as understanding relevant legal, ethical, and policy issues related to healthcare practice. We didn't talk on the phone until the end of the week, when we would discuss what we had learned and address any areas of uncertainty. This approach helped us stay accountable to each other, and the rule of focusing on one concept per day ensured that we grasped the material thoroughly before moving forward.

Do you know, after studying separately but collectively, we both took our certification exams on the same day—and we both passed!

Maintaining close connections with like-minded peers or mentors who share similar ambitions can provide valuable social support to stay driven.

Reflection time:

1. How do your surroundings, both physical and social, influence your motivation and productivity?

   _____

   _____

   _____

2. Have you ever found inspiration or motivation from being in a space where others are also working toward their goals, even if you didn't know them personally?

   _____

   _____

   _____

3. What steps can you take to create or find an environment that supports your goals and makes you feel connected to others on a similar path?

   _____

Dr. Kim Anderson

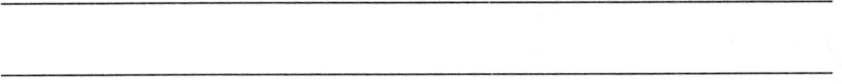

CHAPTER NINETEEN

TURNING FEAR INTO FUEL: USING ANXIETY AS MOTIVATION

I'll be honest—at some point, we've all experienced fear. For me, it often came from the unknown, the "what ifs." I'd wonder, "What will I do? How will I make it through? Can I even survive this?" It's almost like I got worked up before anything even happened, or I prepped myself for the worst. But looking back now, having moved past it, I agree with Jon Gordon (2020), F.E.A.R. is nothing more than "False Evidence Appearing Real" (p. 1).

I remember when I was preparing for a big exam, and I kept hearing from peers in different classes that the course was incredibly difficult. They shared stories about how hard the test was, and I started to believe that it would be the same for me. I began to worry and doubt myself, thinking, 'If it was tough for them, it will surely be tough for me too.' But when the time came to take the test, I realized something important: just because it was hard for them didn't mean it would be the same for me. I had to remind myself that everyone's

73

experience is unique, and there are many factors that contribute to it. For instance, how did they prepare for the test, or did they prepare at all? The test wasn't as difficult as I had imagined, and I passed with confidence. It was a lesson in understanding that fear often comes from comparing my journey to others—and that doesn't define my own path.

The fear and anxiety surrounding the thought of failing motivated me to go the extra mile. Although I was uncertain about the outcome, I wanted to ensure that I could say I gave it my best effort. I did not want to look back and feel that I could have performed better had I applied myself more. I wanted to walk away from the test knowing that I had done everything in my power. Rather than allowing fear to hinder me, I used it as a catalyst to eliminate any potential roadblocks to my success. I devoted myself to studying thoroughly, supplemented my learning by watching educational videos, created numerous note cards to reinforce key concepts, and even listened to lectures during my commute. I also began to speak life into my situation, reminding myself daily, "I can do all things through Christ who strengthens me" (Philippians 4:13KJV). I chuckle now as I remember saying "I'm going where I must go even when inwardly felt unsure of myself and even afraid." Just saying it, affirming what

I believed fueled my determination and strengthened my resolve.

Let's take a moment to reflect on where we are:

1. What obstacles in your life have you viewed as roadblocks, and how can you shift your perspective to see them as opportunities for growth?

    _____

    _____

    _____

2. Think about a time when you compared your journey to someone else's. How did that affect your mindset, and how can you focus more on your unique path moving forward?

    _____

    _____

    _____

3. What affirmations or positive statements can you implement in your life to help you overcome challenges and stay focused on your goals?

    _____

    _____

    _____

CHAPTER TWENTY

GRATITUDE AS A CATALYST FOR GROWTH

As challenging as things were, the Lord knows they were. I had many sleepless nights, cried countless tears, and at times felt like giving up. There were moments when it felt like no one understood me, and I questioned whether I could keep going. Yet, through it all, I still felt a deep sense of gratitude. I was thankful because I was in high pursuit of my dreams, chasing something I wanted so desperately. I was grateful for the opportunity I had been given—an opportunity that perhaps someone else had been denied. I imagine some may feel like it's no big deal if you don't get in, but when it's tied to your purpose, you hold on tight. You can't let it slip by. For me, this wasn't just about an opportunity—it was about the chance to truly pursue what mattered most and to build a future that aligned with my deepest goals. Being a part of this journey felt like a true honor, and no matter what happened, I made a point to thank God every step of the way because I knew it was only because of His grace that I was here. That sense of gratitude became the driving force behind my perseverance. I learned to stop complaining. If I couldn't say anything positive, I chose to just remain quiet. Instead, I focused on giving my best and trusting the process.

Practicing gratitude has a remarkable way of shifting your mindset. When we focus on what we are thankful for, even during difficult times, it shifts our perspective. Instead of dwelling on what's hard or what's missing, we begin to appreciate the progress we've made and the opportunities we have. This shift in focus can help accelerate our progress toward our goals because it fosters resilience, positive energy, and a deeper sense of purpose. Gratitude reminds us that even in the face of adversity, we have something to be thankful for— and that awareness can push us to keep moving forward with renewed determination.

Let's look inward for a moment.

1. When facing challenges, how can you shift your focus from what's difficult to what you're grateful for?

_____

_____

_____

2. Think about a time when you felt misunderstood or alone in your journey. How did you overcome those feelings, and what did you learn from the experience?

_____

_____

_____

3. In what ways can practicing gratitude help you push through obstacles and keep pursuing your goals, even when the road gets tough?

_____

_____

_____

CHAPTER TWENTY-ONE

LESSONS FROM THE DETOUR

The detour was painful — not because I didn't want to move forward, but because I just didn't know where I was headed. I knew where I wanted to be. I had vision. I had dreams. I made attempts to get there… but life was *lifeing*. I lost my mother. I lost my marriage. I lost my job. And in the midst of it all, It felt like I lost *me*.

But through that pain, God was working. The Lord was crushing me, breaking me — not to destroy me, but to transform me into who He predestined me to be. I can still remember moments where it felt like I was dying… not physically, but spiritually. The old me was being stripped away.

God had to remove what no longer fit where He was taking me. It's like this: imagine a prince showing up in a limousine to take you to a 5-star dining experience. Torn jeans, a ragged t-shirt, and run-over shoes just won't do. That kind of atmosphere requires a different preparation, a different presentation.

And that's what God was doing with me — preparing me for where He was taking me.

So, the detours weren't just delays — they were necessary stops.

Stops where I had to unload some baggage that wasn't meant to come with me:

Bitterness, wrath, anger, clamor, and evil-speaking be put away from you, with all malice.

Those weights would've slowed me down or even disqualified me from reaching the next destination. The detour became the place where God said, *"You can't take that with you."*

And while I was unloading, He began to help me pick up what I truly needed for the road ahead:

Kindness. Tenderheartedness. Forgiveness. Wisdom. And a deeper trust in Him.

The detour was never about punishment — it was about preparation.

Let's Reflect:

1. What unexpected detours in your life have taught you the most about yourself or your faith journey?

_____

_____

2. What negative emotions or burdens (like anger, jealousy, unforgiveness) have you had to unload to move forward?

3. In what ways did God use a painful season to prepare you for a greater purpose?

CHAPTER TWENTY-TWO

LEGACY IN MOTION

When we think about legacy, we often focus on what we'll leave behind. But I've come to realize that the true essence of legacy is not in what is said about us after we're gone, but in what is being said about us **now**. The Bible tells us that once we leave this life, "the dead remember this life no more" (Ecclesiastes 9:5). This means we won't have control over the words spoken after we're gone.

Therefore, our focus should be on what we are doing today, in this moment, and what others are witnessing and saying about us right now.

But I've learned legacy isn't just something you leave — it's something you live.

It's not built at the finish line — it's built in motion, in the journey, in every "yes" to God when "no" would've been easier.

It's built in obedience. In resilience. In faith.

Legacy is what's being written in your everyday decisions, even the unseen ones.

It's how you love. How you forgive. How you rise after falling. How you strive to exhibit the character of God.

It's what your children, your grandchildren, your students, your community will remember long after your titles fade.

I didn't always understand that. I thought I had to arrive at a certain destination before my life would matter — before I could say I was successful, impactful, or even "used by God." But I've come to see that every step, even the missteps, were part of something bigger.

The story of my life has already been written — I am simply walking in the path God has laid out for me — and not just for me.

But for those who would read it.

Those who would watch stumble, fall, and get back up again.

Those who would say, *"If she made it through that, maybe I can too."*

Legacy is in motion.

It's moving through your testimony.

It's showing up in your healing.

It's echoing through every room you walk into and every life you touch.

So, keep going.

Even if the road isn't clear.

Even if you feel unseen.

Even if you're still healing.

Because when you move with God, you're not just building a life —

You're building a legacy.

Let's Reflect:

1. What kind of legacy are you building with your current choices and mindset?

_____

_____

_____

2. Who is watching your journey that might be impacted by your persistence?

_____

_____

_____

3. How can you live more intentionally today, knowing your legacy is being written now?

_____

_____

_____

CHAPTER TWENTY-THREE

IT HAPPENS WHEN YOU DRIVE

When I say, "Drive even though the direction is unclear," what I'm really saying is — go forward. Keep moving. As I reflect on my life, I'm reminded that you could not have told a little girl growing up in poverty — a girl who shared a bed with her sister — that she would one day open her home to resident students from Vietnam, learning their culture and hearing their stories as they pursued medical degrees far from home.

You couldn't have told me that I would one day become a Doctor of Nursing Practice. That I would teach nursing students preparing for their Bachelor of Science in Nursing. That I would one day own my own practice — New Leaf Wellness & Behavioral Health. That I would become a Certified Life Breakthrough Coach, helping others walk in clarity, healing, and purpose.

And you definitely couldn't have told me that after failing my first nursing class and certification, I would still become a Registered

Nurse, a Family Nurse Practitioner, and a Psychiatric Mental Health Nurse Practitioner.

But let me be honest — the road hasn't been easy. I've made mistakes. I've taken wrong turns. I looked for love in all the wrong faces. I married outside of the will of God. I mismanaged money to the point of bankruptcy. I searched for acceptance from others, even though — deep down — I knew God had already accepted me. I longed for validation because I didn't truly know who I was.

And I cry as I say this — I became a parent while I was still a child myself. I wasn't mentally, emotionally, or financially prepared. But God's grace covered me. He carried me through every storm I thought would break me.

I've come to believe that movement leads to destination. Even when I didn't know exactly where I was going, God did. Having those students live with me? That wasn't random — it was preparation. Teaching nursing students now? It's part of my purpose. Every failure, every setback, every "not yet" shaped the woman I've become.

God doesn't waste anything. He takes the broken, overlooked, rejected pieces and builds something beautiful for His glory. He prepares us — even when we can't see it — to fulfill His divine will.

So how does it happen when the direction is unclear?

It happens by faith. It happens when you drive anyway.

Because when God is leading the way, the destination is already written — and victory is guaranteed.

Let's Reflect:

1. What has happened in your life simply because you made the decision to keep moving forward, even when the path wasn't clear?

   _____

   _____

   _____

2. Are there areas in your life right now where fear is keeping you parked, when God is calling you to drive?

   _____

   _____

   _____

3. How can you begin to trust the journey, even without having all the answers or directions?

_____

_____

_____

CHAPTER TWENTY-FOUR

MY BREAKTHROUGH – AND BEYOND

Earning my Doctor of Nursing Practice degree represents more than just academic success—it's the transformation of pain into purpose. This achievement is not only a personal triumph; it's a testament to perseverance, faith, and the relentless drive to rise above every obstacle.

It's a symbol of the unwavering determination and unyielding willpower to keep moving forward, trusting God every step of the way. This degree reflects my journey of pushing through adversity, never giving up, and relentlessly pursuing a better life.

But more importantly, this moment is a reminder for anyone reading this: *Your breakthrough is possible too.* No matter the size of the obstacles in your life, no matter the setbacks you've faced, you are more than capable of overcoming them. I stand here today because I chose not to give up, even when the road felt impossible. You have that same strength within you.

This is proof that with faith, resilience, and an unbreakable spirit, *your breakthrough* will come. Keep pushing. Keep believing. Keep moving forward. The best is yet to come.

Beyond is when you no longer define yourself by what broke you, but by what built you after the breaking. It's the version of you that walks with wisdom, speaks with boldness, and moves with intention. It's the part of your story where you start helping others rise, because you know what it took for you to stand.

Beyond is where clarity meets calling. Where pain becomes purpose. It's where **DRIVE** becomes **destiny**.

Dr. Kim Anderson, DNP-FPA, APRN, FNP-BC, PMHNP-BC

References

Gordon, J. (2020). F. E. A. R. (FALSE EVIDENCE APPEARING REAL). https://people.smu.edu/cgoul/2020/11/14/F-E-A-R-FALSE-EVIDENCE-APPEARING-REAL.

King James Bible. (2024). King James Bible Online. https://www.kingjamesbibleonline.org/ (Original work published 1769).

Lin, Y., Mutz, J., Clough, P.J., Papageorgiou, K.A. (2017). Mental Toughness and Individual Differences in Learning, Educational and Work Performance, Psychological Well-being, and Personality: A Systematic Review. Frontiers in Psychology. https://pmc.ncbi.nlm.nih.gov/articles/PMC5554528/pdf/fpsyg-08-01345.pdf